Plot. Plan. Create.

Unlock Creative Flow and Structure using Noda in Virtual Reality

Michaela Wirtz

Merrywidow Publishing LLC

Virtual reality apps and their client software are updated periodically. There may be some differences between what is presented and what Noda is offering in the future.

ISBN 978-1-969540-00-4 (ebook)

To Brian,

Thank you for building a space where we can think differently,
dream bigger, and create without limits.

wed. A demonic enforcer. Cold and elemental. ner remained nameless, which somehow made him . A forgettable face. Trained to disappear. Arrogant hink obedience comes from blood and chalk.

he notes felt like progress. But the more I added, the see. My desk turned into a patchwork of names and of dialogue, and half-formed rules. Together they noise. I had more fragments than I could manage, them connected.

e point where I used to stall. I pushed the sticky staring at the pile of scraps. None of it connected. I reached for my VR headset and launched the

he Moonroom environment. The lunar base elped spark my creativity.

the middle of the room to give myself plenty n lifted my left arm until the Conversational AI my wrist. "Hey, Pixie," I said. "I need to create three cter arcs."

w minutes describing the characters: the demon dynara, and the would-be sorcerer that I decided described the scene as best as I could, and the al AI went to work.

ted three images and paired each one with a m my ramblings. I followed along as she described r and made some adjustments, then asked her to es and connections.

and talked, the Conversational AI kept refining y time I clarified something, she added another lated a note. I studied the changes as new pieces

Contents

When t
Shows

Some ideas refuse to wai
doing the dishes or falling asl
working on something else.
them or watch them vanish.

This one started with a m
how demons should pity th
summoned them. Most idea
didn't. It circled back again

I kept imagining a smoky
woman tied up in the cente
A furious demonic enforce
the summoner, tall and pai
the circle with more arroga
everything blurred. I only l
alone.

Time to brainstorm. I g
desk and started writing.

Soon, the sticky notes n
name: Zahd. Then a long

Saevin
The su
easier t
enough
At fi
less I co
traits, sc
blurred
and non
This i
notes asi
That's w
Noda ap
I loade
sometime
I move
of space, t
appeared
simple ch
I spent
enforcer, Z
to call Frec
Conversati
She gene
summary f
each charac
add more n
As I pace
the map. Ev
branch or u

appeared, added links where connections made sense, and confirmed that the only outside information she used was story frameworks like the Hero's Journey. Everything else came directly from what I'd given her.

The Conversational AI is designed for brainstorming. She doesn't just capture my notes, she keeps track of them, adds idea nodes as I talk, and turns scattered thoughts into something I can build on.

When I finally stepped back, the Moonroom was full of possibilities. It was more than sticky notes all over my desk. It felt alive. It was only the beginning, but enough to start shaping a rough outline.

I kept walking the map, testing connections and making adjustments, until time slipped away from me and my headset's battery gave out. I exported the map to Miro, pulled the headset off, and checked through data on my computer. Everything from my brainstorming session was there.

The pile of sticky notes wasn't needed. I peeled them off one by one and tossed them into the garbage. No clutter. No second guessing. Just a clear mind and a clean wall.

This is why I use Noda. It mirrors how the creative mind actually works. Not in tidy rows. Not in numbered lists. In loops, clusters, and layers. You don't have to scroll through folders or click through tabs. You just call up the map and walk through it. Spatial memory does the rest.

And it's visually quiet. No endless browser tabs. No inbox trying to get your attention. No phone buzzing with notifications. No interruptions at all. Just you, your voice, your project, and the space to focus.

The best part? You don't have to sit still. You can walk through your map, around it, rearrange ideas mid-thought, and link concepts as they appear. You're inside it your ideas.

That's the real power of VR mind mapping. It gives shape to ideas that arrive too soon, scatter too wide, or refuse to stay quiet. It helps you make sense of the fog before you have a plan. It helps you trust what you already know.

You don't need to be writing fantasy characters for this to matter. Maybe your idea is a course outline, a business pitch, or research that won't fit in a single document. The process is the same: capture the sparks, give them space, and let structure grow around them.

The next time an idea shows up before you're ready, don't try to wrangle it into a spreadsheet or a document. Don't tape it to the wall. Grab your VR headset and step into your next project.

Getting to Know Noda

So, WHAT MAKES NODA more than just another brainstorming tool?

Most creative work happens in two dimensions: screens, notebooks, sticky notes, Kanban boards, even Notion. These tools help us capture ideas, but they don't reflect how we actually think. Ideas don't arrive in neat lines. They come in loops, branches, and clusters. Noda takes you into a space where you can finally work that way.

Noda is a visual mind-mapping app built for virtual reality. You create floating elements, called nodes, and link them into dynamic structures. A node can hold whatever you need to see clearly: an idea, a theme, a timeline, a cluster of research, or even a vocabulary word paired with its image. Instead of flipping between tabs or scrolling through lists, you can spread everything out in one shared space and look around.

You can zoom in on a single detail or zoom out to see the full scope of a project. If something's in the wrong place, grab it and move it. Want to track timelines, emotional beats, or shifting priorities? Change a node's color, shape, or position, or even add an image. The space becomes a visual memory system that's easier to recall and refine.

Some people build methodically. Others start messy and sort it out along the way. There's no single right way to map. Noda adapts to your process.

It also comes with built-in AI support, designed to enhance rather than replace your creativity. Lift your left wrist and you'll see the conversational AI assistant. Give her a prompt and she creates nodes that capture your request, often asking guiding questions to refine your ideas. You can generate quick visuals to anchor a node, or create pros-and-cons lists to weigh a choice. The AI doesn't replace imagination. It extends it, turning fragments into fuller ideas, surfacing new directions, and keeping momentum when you're stuck.

Noda is also collaborative. You and a few coworkers, classmates, editors, or teammates can step into the same map from different locations and lets you talk while you work. The app uses your VR headset's default avatar, so there's no extra setup. Everyone can move, edit, and rearrange ideas in real time. Later, you all have access to the same map so you can keep refining at your own pace.

Need to step away from VR? Export your map as a CSV. It opens as a simple spreadsheet you can sort in Excel or Google Sheets. You'll also get an email with a web link that opens the map in a browser, which is perfect for reviewing or sharing. The browser link is view-only, but you can make changes in the CSV and re-import it into Noda so your map keeps growing.

Once you've used Noda a few times, the workflow starts to feel natural. Launch the app in your headset, open a map or a meeting room, and begin laying out ideas. You move through the space with controllers or hand tracking.

Writers use Noda to trace character arcs and story beats. Students prepare for exams and organize material. Teams plan projects and track milestones. Researchers connect sources into patterns they might have missed on paper. Families map their history across generations. Designers sketch user journeys and feature flows. And decision-makers lay out options, weigh trade-offs, and move forward with confidence.

Like any creative environment, Noda has its limits: it runs only in VR, offers no preset templates, and asks you to build your own system. There's a short learning curve, but once you find your rhythm the tool fades and the ideas take over.

And that's the point. Noda isn't the place to write your project. It's not a replacement for planning software, task boards, or editing tools. It's what you use first, when the shape of the project hasn't revealed itself yet.

Once you walk through your ideas, see your structure in full view, and move things around with your own hands, it's hard to go back to a flat screen. Let's get you building.

First Steps

STEP ONE: DOWNLOAD THE app to your VR account. The most current and fully supported version is available on the Meta Quest store. After installing, create your account, confirm your email, and open Noda from your library.

If you're using Noda for the first time, a built-in tutorial called the Tour opens automatically. It walks you through creating nodes, linking them, and moving through space. You can revisit it anytime by selecting Tour from the in-app menu.

Noda also runs on Steam, Viveport, and Oculus Rift, but the Quest version offers the most complete experience. Setup instructions and limitations for other platforms are included in Appendix A.

Before building your first map, it helps to know which account tier you're using, what devices are supported, and how movement works in the virtual space. Every user can begin with a free account, and the current pricing for each tier is outlined below. Since costs may change, you can always confirm the latest details on the Noda website.

Account Options: Free, Core, and Plus

Noda Free – $0/month: Best for newcomers or occasional users.

- Create nodes with text, images, notes, and links
- Autosave
- Group, move, edit, copy, and delete nodes
- AR passthrough (full or edge-only)
- Multiple web browsers with copy/paste and image cropping
- Access to 4 virtual environments
- 3 saved maps
- Up to 50 nodes per map
- 1 binaural beats track
- 1 minute/day of speech-to-text
- 45 minutes/month of multi-user time
- Lifetime limit of 25 AI image credits

Noda Core – $29.99 one-time purchase: Great for creators who want expanded functionality without a subscription.

- Everything in the Free tier
- Access to 8 environments

- Unlimited saved maps and nodes
- 4 binaural tracks
- CSV import/export
- 60 minutes/month of speech-to-text
- 150MB of hosted exports (web map URLs)
- Lifetime limit of 1,000 AI image credits

Noda Plus – $4.99/month: Designed for power users and teams.

- Everything in Core
- Access to 11 environments (with more under consideration)
- Unlimited speech-to-text and export hosting
- Unlimited collaboration time
- 500 AI image credits per month

Controller Basics

Once your account is ready, the next step is learning how to move and interact inside Noda. Controllers are your main tool, although hand tracking lets you work without them.

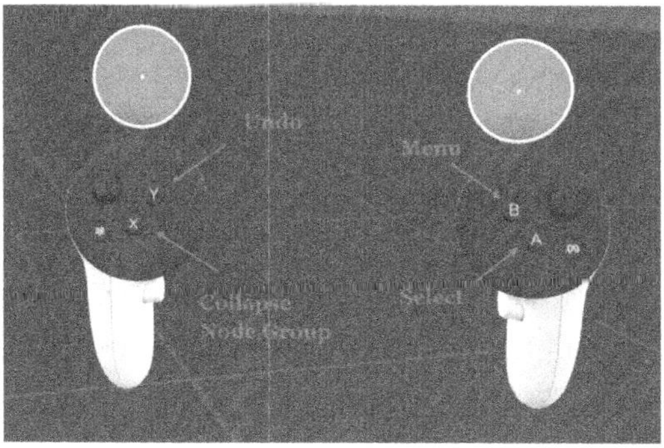

Look at the tip of your controllers. If you are using hand tracking, look just above your fingers. You will see a small white circle. That circle is your pointer and it is the starting point for every interaction. Whether you are creating a node, connecting ideas, or opening a menu, the circle has to be on the object you want to use. Think of it as your cursor in three dimensions.

On the right-hand controller, press **A** to select a node group, press **B** to open the in-app menu, and use the thumbstick to move or rotate. On the left-hand controller, press **X** to collapse node groups and **Y** to undo.

The controls may look simple, but there are a few nuances. To select a group, place the circle inside one of the nodes before pressing **A**. The node flashes to confirm. Hold the trigger and draw a ring around the nodes you want. A white outline appears as you go. Release to confirm, then press the trigger again to open the group menu. From here you can rename, recolor, reshape, add notes, or apply the same image across all nodes.

Groups collapse and expand just as easily. Place the circle inside the main node and press **X**. Connected subnodes fold away, leaving two orbiting dots as a marker. Press **X** again to expand them. Made a mistake? Tap **Y** to undo your last steps until the map looks right again.

Creating and Editing Nodes

Nodes are the heart of every map. To create one, aim the circle where you want it, press and hold the upper trigger, and a green node appears. Keep holding the trigger as you say the name for that node. Words will show above the node in real time, then settle into place as its label. This is the fastest way to work and keeps your flow moving. An in-app keyboard is also available.

You can also launch speech-to-text from the in-app menu by selecting the microphone icon. The virtual keyboard is always there as a backup, but speaking is by far the quickest way to label nodes or add notes.

Editing works much the same way. Place the circle inside a node and squeeze the trigger to open its menu. From there you can dictate changes, add notes, change color or shape, attach an image, or open the in-app browser.

Connections extend your ideas into networks. Place the circle in a node, hold the trigger, and drag the controller to another node. Release to form a link. To move a node, aim inside and press the grip trigger. To resize, bring both hands to the node, align the circles until you see a white outline around it, and pull outward or push inward with the grip triggers. To delete, aim inside, pull the thumbstick down until the circle turns black, and press the trigger. With hand tracking enabled, these same actions can be done with pinches and pulls, letting you create without controllers at all.

At first the hand motions may feel mechanical. Give it time and they become second nature, leaving you free to focus on the ideas. If you would like to see these gestures in action, the Noda YouTube channel offers quick demos.

Moving Around Noda

You can move through Noda in two ways: teleporting or fluid motion. Teleporting is quick and precise. Push the thumbstick forward to create a white line, aim where you want to go, and press the trigger to jump there.

You can also use fluid motion to move around. It feels more natural, like climbing an invisible ladder. Hold the grip trigger, then pull or push your hand in the direction you want to move. Release when you are ready to stop.

Now that you know how to use the controllers and move yourself, let's take a look at the in-app menu.

The Main Menu

THE MAIN MENU IS the control center for everything in Noda. It is where you create maps, adjust settings, join meetings, and shape the space around you.

Press the **B** button on your right controller and the menu appears in front of you. A white pointer beam shows up as your hand or controller moves closer. Point it at a button and use the upper trigger to make a selection.

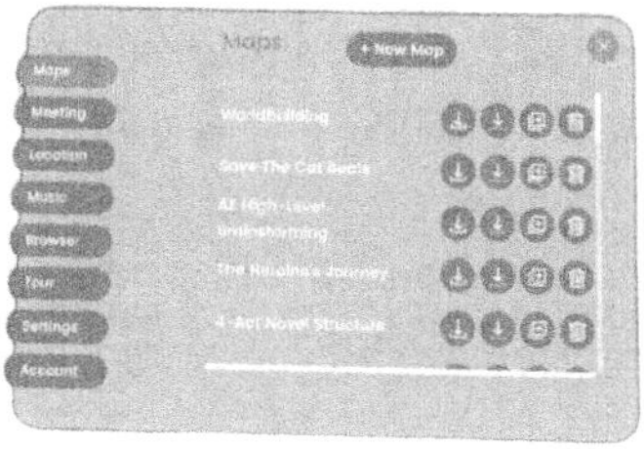

You can also move the menu itself. Aim the pointer at the panel, press the wrist trigger, and drag it wherever it feels most useful. The same method works for other tools such as keyboards and browsers. Place them where they make sense for you and build the workspace that feels natural.

Here is an overview of the main sections of the menu and how you can use them.

The **Maps** tab is where you create and organize your projects. When you open Noda, a starter map is waiting for you, named with the current date. Rename it to match the project you are working on so it is easier to stay organized as you create more maps.

To create a new map, select + **New Map** at the top of the menu. Each map has its own controls:

- Open: Click the Open icon next to a map's name to open it.
- Import: Bring another map into your current one.
- Duplicate: Make a copy of the current map.
- Delete: Remove a map permanently.
- Download: Export your current map as a CSV file (available for Core and Plus users).
- Rename: Click the pencil icon next to the map's name, type a new title, and press Enter.

Each project deserves its own map, especially if you are on a free account with node limits. Keeping maps separate helps you stay immersed in one project at a time without clutter or distraction.

Meetings

Meetings create a space that brings collaboration alive. They are built for working with others on outlines, project plans, study sessions, family trees, or decisions that need more than one perspective. Instead of sitting in a conference room or trying to brainstorm on a video call, you step into the same map and shape ideas together in real time. The result is quicker alignment, more creative energy, and stronger connections.

When you open the Meetings tab, Noda automatically uses your headset's account name, though you can change it at any time. To join, enter the Room Key your team agreed on and click Connect. You will appear in the map and location hosted by the first person who joined. From there, everyone works in the same space, building, editing, and exploring ideas in real time.

Working in a meeting feels different from screen-based collaboration. You are not staring at a grid of faces. You are moving through a shared map, watching ideas emerge around you. It is immersive, interactive, and turns brainstorming into a live experience rather than another call.

Locations

Locations in Noda are more than backgrounds. Each one is an immersive environment designed to shape how you think, plan, and collaborate. Whether you are working solo or with a group, the space around you can influence your energy, focus, and creative rhythm.

When you launch Noda, you enter the last location you used. From there, you can switch to another space that suits your current project, whether that means spreading out a massive map or finding a quiet corner to think through revisions.

All users begin with four free locations, each designed for different project needs. Core users unlock four additional environments with expanded layouts and ambiance. Plus members have three more premium locations to choose from.

Free Environments

- **The Sunroom**: Bright, warm, and inviting. A circular indoor space that opens into a sunlit grove. The interior is ideal for structured maps, while the outdoor space offers room for free exploration.

- **The Grid**: Clean, expansive, and endlessly open. A blank canvas for massive, interconnected maps. Perfect for complex brainstorming or creating step-by-step workflows.

- **VaporWave**: A neon-lit road with glowing palms and a retro-futuristic sunset. Great for maps that evolve in a forward flow, encouraging big-picture thinking.

- **The Classic**: The original Noda space. Simple, compact, and functional, marked with a glowing Noda sign. A nostalgic home base for many users.

Core Environments

- **The Gallery**: Quiet and contemplative, with recessed niches and a balcony. Ideal for breakout groups and layered collaboration.

- **The Hangar**: Dark, moody, and enclosed. Designed for focused work or small-team problem solving without visual distractions.

- **The Moonroom**: A circular chamber with panoramic lunar views, boulders, conference tables, and a hidden corridor. Great for group mapping and side maps.

- **The Stage**: A performance space with seating for fifty and a central area for presenting. Perfect for rehearsals, demos, and structured team sessions.

Noda Plus Environments

- **The WorldRoom**: Spacious and grounded, with a copper world globe and panoramic savanna views. Suitable for strategic mapping and legacy projects.

- **Glasshouse**: Transparent and serene, set in a forest clearing with floor-to-ceiling windows, living areas, and subtle ambient sounds. A calming space to slow down and let ideas breathe.

- **The Art Room**: Modeled after an East Asian art studio, this space is filled with creative energy. Includes painting tables, sculptures, and a tucked-away side room for node clusters.

Choosing the right environment is about more than aesthetics. It is about finding the space that supports the kind of thinking you want to do. Some people settle into one favorite, while others switch depending on the day's project.

Music

The Music tab lets you add sound to your workspace. Noda includes a curated set of binaural tracks from Enlightened Audio, created to support focus, deep thinking, and creative flow. Music is personal, so even in a meeting, only you will hear the track you choose.

Tracks range from 2 to 15 minutes and provide gentle soundscapes for brainstorming, outlining, or mapping ideas. For safety, note that binaural beats are not recommended for users with epilepsy, pacemakers, or photosensitivity. Depending on your plan, you may have access to a sample track or the full library.

- **Adrift**: Calm and spacious, designed for clarity of thought.
- **Mystic Dawn**: Gentle tones that ease you into a focused state.
- **Untold Depths**: Rich, immersive sound for deep concentration.
- **Future Behold**: Expansive and forward-moving, ideal for vision mapping.

Some people play music sparingly, while others let it run in the background. The key is finding the rhythm that best supports your creativity.

Browser

The Browser brings the web into your VR space. It is a lightweight, embedded browser based on Chromium. It's not a full desktop browser, but is powerful enough for most creative workflows.

Browser Basics

Noda lets you open as many individual browser windows as you need. You can move and resize them, type with either a virtual or physical keyboard, and even attach URLs directly to nodes. If you find an image online, you can drop it straight into your map's image library for later use.

You can also log into your cloud-based accounts, such as Google Drive or Dropbox, to open files or resources as needed. Browser windows remain open as you move tools around or switch between different parts of your map, so you never lose your place.

Advanced Integration

For advanced users, Noda includes an Integration API. You can build a simple web page that runs inside the in-app browser and interacts directly with your open map. With basic tools like HTML, CSS, and JavaScript, you can create or update nodes, build custom workflows, and see changes in real time. For more detail, see the GitHub starter kit or Appendix B.

The browser isn't meant to replace your desktop. It's there to keep you focused, so research and creation flow in the same space.

Tour

The Tour is Noda's built-in tutorial. In just a few minutes, you practice creating nodes, linking them, customizing them, and moving through your environment. You also learn how to resize, reposition, and delete nodes, and how to use the thumbstick and grip controls to navigate.

The Tour ends by showing you how to open the Main Menu, turn on music, and restore deleted items using the **X** button. The short walkthrough is designed to help you build confidence with the core tools before diving into your first project.

Settings

The Settings panel lets you fine-tune how you work:

- **Speech to Text**: Turn voice input on or off.

- **Language**: Choose the language you speak for better voice recognition. Menus remain in English, but recognition improves.

- **Passthrough Mode**: Blend your physical surroundings with your map using your headset's cameras. Use Mode to enable full camera view or a simplified outline view, and adjust brightness.

- **Spatial Anchors**: Lock your map to a specific spot in your physical space so it appears in the same place every time. Anchors are set per map and can be placed, activated, shown, or cleared. Spatial anchors work best on headsets that support passthrough and room tracking. When this feature is active, your map does not just exist in VR. It stays exactly where you left it.

- **Console**: A tool for advanced users who want to run scripts or work with Noda's WebAPI. It shows live system messages inside your workspace. See Appendix B for more detail.

- **In-App Camera**: Record directly inside Noda. A virtual camera appears with options to view, record, flip, and close. Recordings are saved to your headset and can be shared later

Account

The Account tab shows your current membership status and available upgrades. Free accounts display node limits and feature comparisons. Core and Plus members see a summary of their access level and additional tools.

When you first open the Main Menu, it can feel like a lot. Slow down and try one thing at a time. Rename your starter map. Step into a meeting with a collaborator. Switch your location and notice how the space changes your focus.

Each tab is there to give you more control over your ideas, but you don't need to master everything at once. The more time you spend inside the menu, the more natural it becomes. Eventually it stops feeling like a control panel and starts feeling like the doorway to your own creative space.

Mapping Basics

A map in Noda is like a constellation of ideas. Each node can hold a title, notes, links, and images. You can move them around, connect them, spread them out, or pull them closer. Over time, your map stops feeling like a tool and starts feeling like a place you built for yourself: part workspace, part memory palace, part creative playground.

All maps are saved to your account. You can open, rename, duplicate, or delete them whenever you like. Free accounts allow up to three maps. Core and Plus members can create as many as they need. Each map develops its own rhythm, its own spatial logic, and its own story.

At the heart of every map are two components: nodes and links.

Nodes

Nodes are the building blocks of every map. Creating one is simple: aim your pointer, press the trigger, and a green node appears. From there you can name it, move it, style it, or connect it. Every map, no matter how complex, starts here.

- **Move a node**: Place the white circle inside the node and use the grip trigger to drag it into position. With hand tracking, just reach out and grab the node. To resize, use both hands. With controllers, squeeze the grip triggers while you move. With hand tracking, stretch or compress the node until it is the size you want.

- **Delete a node**: Place the white circle inside the node, pull the thumbstick back until the circle turns black, and press the trigger to confirm.

- **Open the node menu**: Place the white circle inside the node and pull the upper trigger. This in-app menu is the gateway to every other change: naming, color, shape, notes, images, pages, and links. From this point forward, any time you want to adjust a node, you'll do it through the node menu.

You can name nodes in two ways:

- **Speech-to-text**: Point at the microphone icon in the submenu. Place the white circle inside the node and hold the upper trigger. A glowing line appears above the node, showing speech-to-text is active. Speak clearly and your words appear in real time. Release the trigger to stop recording.

- **Typing**: Place the white circle inside the node and pull the upper trigger. The in-app node menu will appear. Point your finger or controller at the input field marked "Node." A virtual keyboard appears. Enter a title and click **Done** to save it.

Naming quickly keeps your flow moving. Whether you speak or type, the point is to label your idea before it drifts.

Color

The Color tab offers 36 shades to choose from.

- **Change a node's color**: Select a shade and apply it.
- **Use color for structure**: Assign colors to categories, stages, or themes so patterns stand out.

Colors become shortcuts that your brain remembers, making it easier to scan a dense map at a glance.

Shape

The Shape tab offers several designs for sorting, grouping, or prioritizing information.

- **Change a node's shape**: Pick from the available options.
- **Use shapes with color**: Combine them to build a visual shorthand for categories, tasks, or characters.
- **Access AI tools**: Two Brain icons appear here. Tap one to activate Pixie, which can expand the node with brainstorming ideas or create a quick pros-and-cons list.

Shapes add another layer of meaning: a triangle, square, or circle can signal what a node represents before you even read the text.

Images

The Image tab lets you add visual anchors to your map. You can use emojis, saved images, or generate new ones with AI.

- **Add an emoji**: Choose the emoji icon to replace the node shape.

- **Add a saved image**: Select the photo icon, and choose from images stored in this map.

- **Bring in an image from the web**: Open the in-app browser, point at an image, pull the trigger, and drag it into your map. It is saved to this map's image files.

- **Generate an image with AI**: Select the Brain icon. Pixie uses the node's title, notes, and links to create options. Select Refresh to see new variations. Credits appear at the bottom of the panel.

- **Replace or remove**: Choose another image, emoji, or none.

- **Resize and position**: Resize the node itself and the image scales with it. Move it anywhere with the grip trigger or hand tracking.

Important note: images are saved per map. They do not carry over to other projects.

Notes

The Notes tab lets you expand a node with longer text.

- **Add a note by speaking**: Point at the microphone icon and talk clearly. Your words appear in the text box.

- **Add a note by typing**: Point at the entry field to bring up the virtual keyboard, or use a connected wireless keyboard for faster input.

Notes keep context close. You can outline an idea, capture research, or add reminders without leaving the map.

Page

The Page tab opens Noda's built-in browser. The keyboard appears on the left, and the browser window opens on the right. Type a full URL or use the search bar to look something up.

The browser is ideal for research: pull in references, check sources, log into tools like Google Docs or Slack, or even use AI assistants. Audio isn't supported, so you can't make video calls, but most text-based platforms work well.

The advantage is that everything stays inside your workspace. You don't need to take off the headset, break concentration, or lose your flow.

Links

Links transform a cluster of nodes into a structured map. They reveal relationships, hierarchies, and sequences so you can see how ideas connect. A map without links is just a floating collection of thoughts. A map with links becomes a network of meaning.

- **Create a link**: Place the circle inside a node, hold the trigger, drag to another node, then release. A thin black line appears. The first node becomes the main node and the second becomes a subnode.

- **Collapse groups**: Order matters. When you collapse a group, subnodes hide beneath the main node. This is how you cluster and streamline large maps.

- **Customize links**: Place the circle on a connector line and press the trigger to open the link menu. Options appear to add a label, change color, adjust line style or thickness, add curves, or include motion.

Styled links are not just decoration. They create rhythm and emphasis, making dense maps easier to read and more satisfying to build.

From Nodes and Links to Narratives: Structuring Your Map

Now that you know how to create and customize nodes, you can start shaping ideas into something bigger. Structure brings coherence, and you can build it through clustering, sequencing, and hierarchy.

- **Clustering** groups related ideas in the same space. Writers might cluster character traits or story beats. Students can gather supporting details around a concept. Coaches can arrange learner insights to show patterns. Clusters make maps easier to scan and navigate.

- **Sequencing** shows order and flow. Writers might map a story arc. Students can show steps in an argument. Educators can build lesson plans. Sequencing gives momentum and turns loose thoughts into a clear path.

- **Hierarchy** emphasizes importance. Place central ideas in the middle or top, branch out with supporting points, and use colors or line weights to show priority. Writers show weight and focus, students outline arguments, and coaches highlight priorities.

These strategies rarely appear in a set order. You might cluster first and then notice a sequence, or you might build a sequence that reveals a hierarchy. Most maps evolve through a mix of all three.

Keep adjusting as you go. Split clusters that feel crowded. Pull stray nodes toward the ideas they support. Use color, size, and placement to bring key points forward.

There is no single right way to structure a map. Aim for clarity, not perfection. Think of your map as a launchpad. Step inside it, walk through the patterns you've built, and notice how your ideas feel different when you see them connected in space. A structured map is not the final product. It's a foundation you can return to as your ideas keep growing.

Pixie and the Brains

Most people use AI tools like ChatGPT for quick results. They ask for outlines, summaries, or email drafts, and the AI delivers polished content in seconds. For many, it's a shortcut and is more about speed than discovery.

Instead of giving you a completed product, Noda's AI helps you lay a foundation. It offers four modes: **Conversational**, **Brainstorming**, **Pros and Cons**, and the **Image Generator**. The first three are designed to expand your map. They don't hand you answers. They nudge you forward, suggest new angles, and spark connections you might have missed.

Conversational AI Assistant

Noda's Conversational AI sits at the heart of the system. I nicknamed her the **Pixie**. She's one of the most powerful features in Noda, and she changes what's possible in VR. Instead of typing prompts into a flat screen, you talk to her in real time, from inside your map, and she helps you shape what you're building. Once you get used to working with her, it's hard to imagine brainstorming without her.

The Pixie lives just above your left wrist. Raise your arm and she appears over the status indicator. This display shows her current state (ready, sending, working, or verbalizing) along with how long she's been working with you.

Next to her, the phrase *pinch to talk* reminds you how to activate her. Pinch your thumb and forefinger together, or press and hold the upper trigger while you speak. Once you're done, release the trigger, and the Pixie gets to work.

Most AI tools require rigid, role-based prompts. You set tone, length, and persona. Noda's Conversational AI works differently. She's not here to give you polished content. She explores with you. She maps your ideas, follows threads, and helps you shape something that is still taking form.

When I asked her how to get the best results, the Pixie kept it simple. These are her own words:

- **Ask questions.** If you're unsure about the process, ask me to clarify.

- **Use descriptive language.** Names, colors, shapes, and locations guide me to create what you're aiming for.

- **Request visualization.** If you want images or visual elements, say so.

- **Give feedback in iterations.** If the first response misses the mark, tell me what to change.

- **Group multiple requests.** Several tasks can be handled more efficiently together.

- **Engage in dialogue.** Keep the back-and-forth going to reach the best outcome.

Her advice is clear: give her detail, context, and feedback, and she'll help you move your ideas forward. The goal isn't perfection. It's momentum, one idea at a time.

Working with Spoken Prompts

Noda's Conversational AI responds to spoken input, so a little preparation goes a long way. Draft your prompt in a node note or a cloud service such as Google Drive, Dropbox, or OneDrive, then open that file in Noda's in-app browser so it is easy to glance at while you work in VR.

Raise your wrist to bring up the Pixie, pinch to talk or press and hold the upper trigger, and read your prompt aloud. If the request is long, break it into short steps, starting with the basics and layering in more detail as you go. From there, the process becomes conversational. Once the AI generates a response, respond in natural language: "That is close, but add another branch for accessibility needs," or "Color Motivations green instead of blue." In practice, it feels less like issuing commands and more like shaping ideas together until the map matches your vision.

The Pixie also lets you choose how she responds. By default, she explains the nodes she creates and offers context and suggestions for how to use them. If you want a different style, tell her. You can ask her not to explain, to summarize briefly, to create specific kinds of links, or to focus on images first. These preferences are not fixed. They evolve as you use her and learn how you want her to work with you.

Front-loading works best. Start by telling the Conversational AI what you are building and how you want it structured. The more direction you give at the start, the better the first pass.

Layered Prompt Example:

- Create a central node called *User Experience Profile*. Add branches for *Player Types*, *Motivations*, *Emotions*, and *Frustrations*. Color Player Types blue, Motivations green, Emotions yellow, and Frustrations red. Place the branches evenly around the center.

- Now, expand the *Motivations* branch into *Intrinsic* and *Extrinsic*. Under Intrinsic, add subnodes for curiosity, mastery, and creativity. Under Extrinsic, add subnodes for rewards, competition, and recognition. Link both Intrinsic and Extrinsic back to Player Types.

- Add an image to each Player Type node. Use a compass for Explorer, a trophy for Competitor, a book for Storyteller, and a puzzle piece for Problem-Solver. Place the images inside the nodes so they act as quick visual anchors.

The Brains

Pixie is not the only way AI helps. Once you have created a node and added a basic idea, you can ask the AI to take it further. This is useful when you feel stuck, when you are unsure what comes next, or when you want to test a new angle.

Point your white circle into the node and press the **B button** to open the in-app submenu. Select **Shape**, then point at the brain icon and pull the trigger. From there you will see two choices: **Brainstorm Node**, which develops new directions from your starting idea, and **Pros/Cons Node**, which creates a two-column tree to help you weigh a decision.

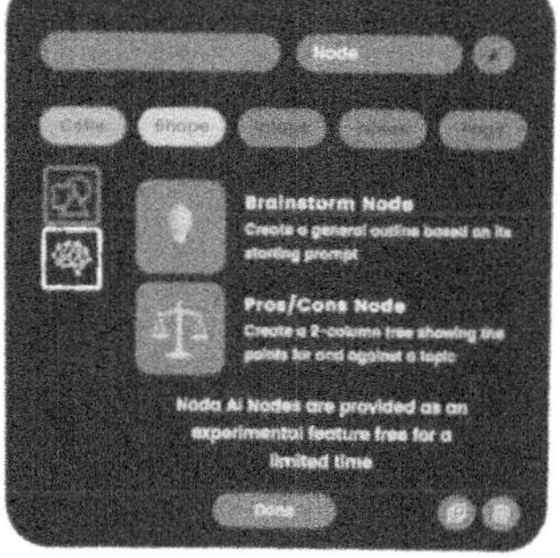

Brainstorming Mode

A Brainstorming node creates a general outline based on your starting prompt: whatever you placed in the main node. The AI generates several subnodes, each with its own offshoots.

This mode is built to spark creative thinking, not limit it. Suggestions may feel overly broad at first or wander in directions you don't expect. That's the point. You can edit, move, or link them however you like. Whether you're mapping a story, building a strategy, or exploring something in between, this is a fast way to build momentum.

Here's what that looked like in practice. I was mapping a character arc for Zahdynara, the Fae Crown Princess. I began with a single note: she's a changeling swapped with her half-human cousin, Elzpeth. Zahdynara never feels like she belongs. Even a light breeze can sting her skin and she's allergic to iron.

When I asked the Brainstorming AI to help, it suggested broad topics like early life, legacy, and impact on the world. Standard directions, but nothing that fully captured the Fae. I followed the thread anyway. Under early life, I added that she was homeschooled, spoke early, and walked late. Most importantly, I noted that she doesn't know she's Fae.

That opened the map in a new direction. I created a node for Fae characteristics, and the Brain suggested prompts for physical appearance, magical abilities, and known behaviors. Those gave me a foothold. From there I imagined Zahdynara undergoing surgery as a toddler to round her pointed ears. I added that her unusual skin sensitivity was dismissed by doctors as a genetic disorder, and that she had to wear specific fabrics just to function comfortably in the human world.

That's the difference. Noda's AI doesn't finish your thoughts; it helps you uncover them. It responds through nodes rather than a chat box, so the way you frame your input matters as much as the ideas themselves.

Brainstorming Prompts

The Brain works best when you give it context. The more information you provide, the better the results.

Steps for effective brainstorming:

1. **Define your focus:** Decide what you want to explore. Is it a theme, a character arc, or a marketing plan? Give yourself a one-sentence objective.

2. **Create your main node:** Give it a short, single-sentence title. Add notes with keywords, goals, tone, or constraints. You can also add an image to guide the AI.

3. **Activate brainstorming:** Point at the lightbulb icon next to 'Brainstorming Node' to activate the AI. This will begin to generate connected subnodes.

4. **Review and refine:** Rename nodes, remove irrelevant ones, and expand the ideas that resonate.

5. **Build:** Add follow-up nodes and re-activate the Brain from those points. Use Pros and Cons on individual subnodes to branch in new directions, if needed.

6. **Organize visually:** Use colors, shapes, or layout to group promising ideas. Visual structure makes connections easier to spot.

7. **Keep experimenting:** Look over the current results, adjust, and learn what kinds of prompts work best.

Pros and Cons Analysis Mode

This mode helps you weigh a decision by breaking it into potential positives and negatives. It's a simple way to compare options and get a clearer view of what's at stake. The AI isn't here to make the decision for you. It gives you a starting point and helps organize your thinking.

When you activate this mode, the AI creates two main nodes, one for **Pros** and one for **Cons**. Each has its own subnodes with high-level points related to the idea you're working on. You can expand, rearrange, or edit each entry as needed. You can also run the AI on any subnode to keep digging into a specific angle.

Here's an example from one of my maps. Prince Cynfael has to decide whether to tell Zahdynara the truth: that she was swapped with her cousin to protect her from danger. On the surface it looks like a single choice, but there's much more underneath.

When I opened the Pros and Cons tool, the AI created the two main nodes. Under **Cons**, it listed complicated family dynamics, the risk of hurting Zahdynara, and the possibility she might see it as betrayal. Under **Pros**, it offered protection, safety, and the value of honesty.

From there, I added my own details. On the Pros side, I noted that the truth could explain Zahdynara's physical struggles and her lifelong sense of disconnection. On the Cons side, I added that she might not believe him, which would only deepen her distrust.

That's when the story started to shift. Until that moment, Cynfael had been a supporting character. As I worked through his decision, deeper questions emerged. Why was he banished to the human world? Why would he surrender his own daughter and raise his niece instead? How would that choice shape the way he treated Zahdynara? Which parts of her identity came from being raised by him?

To keep exploring, I switched back to Brainstorming and let the map expand again.

Pros and Cons Prompts

The Brain can generate pros and cons automatically, but it works best when you set it up clearly. The more context you provide, the sharper and more useful the results.

Steps for effective pros and cons mapping:

1. **Add context:** Include goals, constraints, or considerations. Attach images or diagrams if useful.

2. **Activate Pros/Cons:** Point at the **balance scales icon** next to *Pros/Cons Node* and pull the trigger to activate the AI. This generates two main nodes, one for Pros

and one for Cons, each with connected subnodes.

3. **Review and refine:** Keep what's useful, remove what isn't, and add details where needed.

4. **Compare visually:** Seeing pros and cons side by side helps you weigh trade-offs and spot patterns.

5. **Add nuance:** Expand subnodes, re-run the AI, or switch to Brainstorming for deeper exploration.

6. **Validate:** Double-check facts and details. In fiction, make sure emotional logic holds. In nonfiction, confirm with trusted sources.

One last note: always validate what you get from Noda's AI. All AI systems hallucinate and invent details. If you're writing fiction, make sure the emotional logic holds. If you're working on nonfiction or historical research, confirm names, dates, definitions, and citations against reliable sources.

Noda's AI features are unique in VR. They aren't an add-on or a gimmick. They're built into the way you create, and they're designed to expand what you can do in the moment. Whether you're a writer, a teacher, a student, or a strategist, Noda's AI makes your map more than a static set of nodes. It can help you brainstorm in real time, inside a space built for ideas.

From 3D to 2D

WORKING IN NODA GIVES you the freedom to think in three dimensions, but sometimes you need your ideas in a more traditional format. Maybe you want to collaborate with a team on a Miro board, make bulk edits in a spreadsheet, or keep a portable file you can share outside of VR. Here's how you can move your maps from 3D to 2D without breaking your flow. We'll learn to sync directly with Miro, export and import CSV files, and even transfer files straight to your headset. The result is flexibility. Your ideas move with you, no matter what screen you're working on.

Working with Miro & Noda

Sometimes you just need to move your work between VR and your desktop. Noda gives you the flexibility to brainstorm and build in immersive 3D space, while Miro makes it easy to share, collaborate, and organize on a flat screen. Linking the two lets you shift between immersive creation and practical planning without losing momentum.

Before you begin, you'll need a Noda Plus subscription and a Miro account. The free version of Miro works fine. You'll also need to install the Noda plugin from the Miro Marketplace into the Miro board that you'd like to sync with your Noda map.

To set up the connection, put on your Meta Quest headset and launch the Noda app open to the map you want to sync. Open the in-app browser, visit the Miro website, and log in. Once you are signed in, open the board you want to sync between Miro and Noda.

In the plugin you can choose **Sync Continuously** or **Sync Selected**. Sync Continuously mirrors ongoing changes between your Noda map and your Miro board for as long as your session is active. Sync Selected works differently. When you highlight objects in either Noda or Miro, the Sync button in the plugin becomes active. Pressing the blue Sync button copies only those selected items to the other side.

Keep your Miro board open in Noda's in-app browser while you work. If the board closes or your headset goes idle, the connection will drop and you'll need to log in again.

Only sticky notes and nodes sync between Noda and Miro. Text boxes, shapes, and images do not transfer. For the smoothest workflow, keep both apps open and active, and expect to do a little cleanup if your notes include unusual formatting or special characters.

This workflow is most useful when you switch between solo brainstorming and group input. You might begin in Noda, laying out ideas quickly with speech-to-text and moving nodes around until they make sense. When you're ready for feedback, sync those nodes into Miro so your team can comment and build with you. Or you can go the other way: start with sticky notes on a Miro board during a meeting, capture your group's thoughts, and then send those notes into Noda to see how they connect in 3D.

Either direction works. The point is that you're never locked into one format. Writers use this to brainstorm a draft in VR and then share an outline with their editor in Miro. Coaches capture group sessions as sticky notes and bring them into Noda to reveal hidden themes. Educators collect student responses on a Miro board and then explore those ideas in 3D with the class. The flow is flexible, and you're free to move between spaces without losing your momentum.

Export and Import with CSV

Not every workflow requires Miro. Noda also works with CSV files (Comma Separated Values), which makes it possible to move your maps into other tools, make bulk edits, or share a read-only version of your map with someone who does not use Noda. Keep in mind that a CSV file is only a snapshot in time. If changes are made after the export, they will not appear in the CSV. For the most accurate version, always load the current map in Noda.

Every CSV exported from Noda contains all the fields needed to recreate a map. The first line of the file is a header row that labels the fields, and each subsequent line represents a node and its details. For importing, the only required field is the Name or Title column. This flexibility means you can edit as much or as little as you want. Some users simply rename nodes, while others restructure entire projects in a spreadsheet before bringing them back into Noda.

Exporting a Map

To export, open the in-app menu and go to **Maps**. Open the map you want to export, then click the **Export (CSV)** icon for that map. A submenu appears asking for your email address. Once you confirm, Noda sends you an email with both a browser link and a downloadable CSV file.

From there, you can choose how to work. Opening the browser link lets you zoom, pan, and review your structure visually. It's a quick way to check your layout before moving into a spreadsheet or outline. Opening the CSV file in a spreadsheet editor makes it easy to bulk edit, rename nodes, rearrange items, or add and remove content outside of VR.

Imagine a research student exporting their notes into CSV, reorganizing data into categories, and then pulling it back into Noda to visualize connections. Or a project manager renaming tasks in bulk from Excel before syncing back into VR for the team's next session. CSV makes those workflows practical.

Importing a Map

Save the updated CSV file to a cloud storage service like Google Drive or Dropbox. Next, log into Noda. Open the in-app menu and choose **Browser**. Sign in to your cloud storage account and locate the file. Click **Download** to bring it into Noda.

Once the download finishes, the map will open in the map you have open. You can save it with a different name, move nodes around, create new connections, or keep editing.

Direct File Transfers

If you prefer, you can transfer CSV files directly to and from your Quest headset. Use either a USB-C cable or AirLink connection to access your device's

storage. The base location for imports and exports is:
\Android\data\com.codingleap.noda\files

Placing a CSV file into this directory makes it available in your Maps menu the next time you open Noda.

Troubleshooting: If Your Map Doesn't Appear

If your map doesn't show up after an import, here are a few things to check:

- **Confirm the file type.** Noda only accepts properly formatted CSV files exported from Noda. If you opened the file in Excel and saved it as .xlsx or another format, it won't import.

- **Check your download.** Make sure you downloaded the file instead of only previewing it. In services like Google Drive, clicking a file may just open a preview window rather than saving the file to your device.

- **Refresh the Maps menu.** Close the menu, reopen it, and check again. Sometimes the new file doesn't display until the menu reloads.

- **Re-export if needed.** If edits break the formatting, return to your original Noda export, make smaller changes, and try again.

These small checks usually solve the problem and get your map visible again.

Bringing your maps from 3D to 2D gives you flexibility without breaking your flow. Whether you're syncing with Miro for team collaboration or exporting a CSV for bulk edits, you can step outside VR when you need to and then return with everything waiting for you.

That freedom to move between dimensions is part of what makes Noda so powerful. You can brainstorm ideas in VR, edit them in a spreadsheet, share them with a team in Miro, and then bring them back into your headset to keep building. The work follows you, shifting forms as needed. Instead of breaking your focus, Noda helps you carry it forward.

Collaboration

When most people think of collaboration, it isn't a simple whiteboard session of old. It's a mix of Slack threads, Teams calls, and shared screens. Someone pulls up a document, others start talking, and the meeting becomes a blur of voices, chat messages, screen shares, and half-finished notes.

With Noda, the setup looks different. The results are more focused, more visual, and far more productive.

Instead of passively watching someone else share a screen, everyone in a Noda meeting has access to the same space. You're not just in the same room. You're in the shared map. Ideas aren't captured and then left to sit in an email chain. They're shaped, connected, and built on in real time. Even after the meeting ends, the map remains live and ready whenever you are. Collaboration becomes a living process instead of a one-hour event.

Joining a Meeting

So how do you actually step into one of these shared spaces? Start by opening the in-app menu and selecting **Meetings**. Enter a **Name**. By default this is your account name, but you can change it to anything that suits the group, like a role, department, or nickname. Then enter a **Room Key**, which works like a meeting ID. Hosts can create a new one; participants use the key provided. Once ready, click **Connect** to join the space.

When you connect, the room opens like a workshop that everyone can walk into. Instead of one person driving while the others watch, every participant can create, move, and link nodes. Anything you add appears instantly for everyone else. You're not watching someone else's cursor. You're contributing in real time.

It helps to decide ahead of time who will host the main map. That person sets up the initial structure, gives it a clear name, and opens it for the meeting. From there, everyone else can add, edit, and shape without duplicating effort.

Once the map is in place, collaboration works best when it's active. One person might outline a process while another links related resources. Someone else can refine the layout so clusters of ideas stay easy to follow. With every action visible, the group can divide tasks while keeping sight of the whole.

The best part is what happens after the meeting ends. Everyone who attended has access to the shared map. That means you can re-enter the map at any time, pick up where you left off, and keep building without losing context. If someone misses the first session, they can still join later, meet a teammate in Noda, and pick up the thread. Collaboration doesn't reset. It continues.

If you plan to share a private map, keep in mind that all participants will gain access. To protect your original, create a copy before the meeting. Another option is to import your private map into the collaboration space as a working version.

This keeps your source intact while the team collaborates on the shared copy.

Spatial Audio

Ideas rarely grow in straight lines, and conversations don't either. In traditional video calls every voice comes through at the same volume, no matter who's speaking to whom. Side conversations get noisy, and details can disappear.

Noda works differently. Its audio is spatial, which means voices behave the way they do in the real world. If someone is close to you in the virtual environment, you'll hear them clearly. As they move away, their voice fades naturally.

This design creates room for organic collaboration. Want to break off into a smaller group? Step aside with a few teammates and keep talking. Had a breakthrough and need to share? Walk back toward the main group and your voice rises again. Instead of cutting across one another in a single channel, conversations in Noda flow the way they do in person.

Passthrough Options

Meetings in VR can feel deeply immersive, which is both a strength and a challenge. Sometimes you want the sense of full presence; other times you need to stay grounded in your physical surroundings.

That's where passthrough helps. Open the in-app menu, tap **Settings**, and select **Passthrough**. In **Full** mode your real-world environment appears alongside the nodes and participants. In **Partial** mode you'll see a soft outline of your space, enough to stay oriented without breaking immersion. You can switch between modes at any point in a meeting, depending on what you need.

Preparing for Success

Because meetings happen in real time and in real space, preparation makes a big difference. A little planning up front saves frustration later.

- **Share the agenda.** Ask participants to keep it visible during the session by loading it in their in-app browser. This way the map stays focused on ideas, not on logistics.

- **Know your limit.** Meeting length and node count depend on the lowest-tier participant. If even one person is on the Free or Core plan, the session ends after 45 minutes and caps at 50 total nodes. Only groups made up entirely of Plus users can meet without restrictions.

- **Check connections.** A steady internet signal keeps the session smooth. PCVR setups often handle complex maps and larger groups better than standalone headsets.

- **Plan around access.** CSV import, export, and file sharing are available to Core and Plus users. Confirm who has which plan before relying on shared files. Remember that CSV exports are static snapshots. If changes are made after the export, they won't appear in the file.

- **Be strategic with maps.** Complex projects can sprawl. Instead of forcing everything into a single map, split topics into separate maps or sessions. You can switch between maps on the fly if everyone has access to the map.

- **Watch the clock.** If a Free or Core user is present, Noda ends the meeting at exactly 45 minutes. Keep your agenda realistic and leave time to wrap up.

- **Divide and conquer.** Assign roles in advance. One person might structure, another might do real-time research, and a third might refine the layout. That way, everyone contributes in a way that add value.

- **Preserve your originals.** Sharing a private map gives everyone access to edit it. To keep your source safe, make a copy first or add it into the collaboration space as a working version. That way your original stays untouched while the team builds together.

These small steps set the stage for smoother sessions and more effective collaboration.

Why It Feels Different

The difference between Noda and traditional tools isn't just that you can move nodes around in virtual reality. It's the way collaboration feels when everyone is in the same map. Ideas aren't trapped in chat logs or hidden in someone's slides. They float in front of you. You can walk through them, rearrange them, and watch them shift as the group contributes.

Once you've experienced a meeting where ideas grow in three dimensions and voices carry naturally across the space, it's hard to go back to a static screen. Collaboration in Noda doesn't just produce notes. It creates shared experiences. The map becomes the memory of the meeting, holding the progress and leaving space for the next session to continue.

Whether you're a writing group planning an anthology, a design team refining a product, or a classroom brainstorming ideas, the rhythm is the same. Everyone builds together in the same space, the map holds the progress, and the work continues long after the meeting ends.

Think Like A Power User

If there's one thing power users agree on, it's this: Noda doesn't ask you to change how you work. It adapts to you. The difference is in how they use it. Power users rely on practices that save time, reduce friction, and keep momentum alive. They build reusable patterns with micro maps, keep their flow unbroken with Remote Desktop, share maps to scale ideas, and treat Noda's AI as a partner in shaping their work. These aren't shortcuts. They're systems that help you think faster, build deeper, and stay in flow.

Micro Mapping

Micro mapping is the practice of creating reusable clusters of nodes that give you a roadmap inside larger projects. Instead of starting from a blank canvas every time, you can drop in a ready-made structure and expand from there.

There are two ways to approach micro mapping: creating node type sets and building framework maps.

Node Type Sets

A node type set is the simplest form of micro mapping. By saving single nodes with consistent styles, you create a personal shorthand that makes your maps faster to build and easier to read.

To create one, start by formatting a node with the color, shape, and text you want. Open the node menu by pointing at the node and pulling the upper trigger. Select the pencil icon on the far right. In the Node Type window, give the style a clear name such as "Character," "Location," or "Reference," then click the green checkmark to save.

Once saved, node types become visual shortcuts. A blue diamond might always represent a character, while a green circle signals a deadline. Over time, your brain recognizes these instantly, turning your map into a quick-scan system. Writers often create node types for characters, themes, or conflicts. Project managers build sets for tasks, deadlines, and owners. Educators define objectives, assignments, and assessments. By reusing node types, you create consistency across projects and save time whenever you open a new map.

Framework Maps

The next level of micro mapping is the framework map. Instead of a single node style, this is a small structure you build once and reuse across multiple projects. A framework map acts as a template: a cluster of nodes that lays out a familiar pattern so you don't have to start from scratch.

To create one, begin with a new map and add a central node with the framework's name, such as "Protagonist Arc." From there, create subnodes that represent the steps or elements of the framework. Style them with your saved node types so the map stays visually consistent. When the framework is complete, save the map and keep it on hand as a reusable template for future projects.

One of my own examples is the **Protagonist Arc** Map. At its center is the misbelief or lie the main character carries. Around it I build nodes for the origin of that misbelief, what the character thinks they want, what their true need is, the fear that reinforces the misbelief, and the protective strategies that keep them stuck.

Additional nodes cover the wound or vulnerability that deepens the conflict ahead, the moment of recognition, the decision to change, and the visible transformation. Each time I drop this framework into a new story, I can get to work on a character arc without reinventing the structure.

Share Your Maps

Once you have a framework map that works reliably, you can share it. The same structures that save you time can help others, turning a personal system into something that scales. For power users, maps are more than private tools. They create alignment when others adopt them. Exporting a map extends your workflow to teammates, collaborators, or a wider audience.

I created a framework map called **Fiction Mapping**. It began as my own operating system for story structure, with nodes for plotting tools, brainstorming beats, worldbuilding, and character work. I reused it for every project, always starting with a clean copy and expanding as needed. Eventually, I broke this map into individual pieces and shared it as a reader magnet. What started as a personal system became a resource others could import, adapt, and make their own.

When you share a map, you're not just passing along a file. You're giving someone a way into your process. Make it easy to use. Include a short set of instructions on how to import the map into Noda. Recipients can save the CSV file in their cloud account and import it through Noda's Browser. Once imported, the framework opens as a normal map and can be edited, expanded, or customized like any other.

Sharing maps isn't about giving away your work. It's about multiplying its impact. When you release a framework map, you invite others into your process and give them a proven way to brainstorm. The map becomes more than a tool. It becomes a language others can build with, adapt to their needs, and extend in directions you may not have imagined.

Remote Desktop: The App That Changes Everything

If you're on a Quest headset, install the free **Meta Remote Desktop** app. It lets you bring your computer into virtual reality.

Here's why that matters: brainstorming always turns into writing. Normally, that's the point where you break momentum by taking off your headset and switching to a laptop or tablet, since Noda's built-in browser doesn't cover every tool you need. Remote Desktop bridges that gap.

Stay in Noda, pull up your manuscript or notes, and keep going. No interruption. No re-entry lag. With up to three virtual screens, everything from your computer is right there in front of you.

That continuity is what makes it powerful. You can brainstorm in Noda, draft directly into your manuscript, and return to the map without ever leaving VR. The fewer times you take the headset off, the more momentum you keep.

Remember that Remote Desktop runs as a separate app inside VR. You'll need to toggle back to Noda when you want to edit the map or collaborate. And if you're planning a long session, keep your charging cable close. Running both apps together can drain battery quickly.

Use Noda's Conversational AI Like A Pro

The Pixie works best as a partner, not a shortcut. Give her direction, review what she offers, and build from there. Ask her to rename nodes, add notes, expand ideas, or suggest connections. Each exchange adds momentum to your map.

Refine and Expand Your Ideas

The Conversational AI isn't only for starting fresh. It can help reshape what you already have. Begin with a few nodes, then ask what needs adjusting. A student mapping Social Movements, for example, might refine it into Grassroots Organizing with a note on its role in specific events. The results aren't final answers; they're the raw material. Some suggestions click, others don't, and a few may surprise you into new directions.

It can also grow a single idea into a cluster of related points. Ask the Conversational AI to branch out from Worldbuilding, and it might suggest world rules, geography, cultural norms, historical events, and technology. What begins as a vague parent node becomes a framework you can expand, refine, and rearrange.

Jumpstart Your Stalled Ideas

When you're stuck, even a fragment can give Pixie something to build on. A phrase, mood, or image is often enough. While shaping a scene between Zahdynara and her father, I asked for a metaphor that carried both perspectives. Pixie suggested: eclipse, storm at sea, bird in a cage.

Bird in a Cage reframed the dialogue: for her father, it meant protection; for Zahdynara, it meant prison. That single metaphor reshaped the entire scene around one truth: protection without freedom is still a cage.

Specific input sharpens the output. A well-chosen word can shift a scene, reframe a concept, or open a direction that didn't exist a moment earlier.

Treat AI as Your Partner

Working with the Conversational AI is less about issuing commands and more about conversation. Bring in your goals and context, then react to the suggestions. Ask it to test options, compare approaches, or surface connections. Refine, redirect, and let the map evolve.

Be specific. Vague questions bring vague answers. Explain the purpose of a node or the role of an idea, and you'll get sharper results. Keep the back-and-forth going: ask for refinements, try another angle, or request another round. Feedback makes the partnership stronger.

Even then, remember: The Pixie isn't the author. It moves ideas forward, but the final voice is yours. Power users never confuse the spark for the fire.

Adopt the Power User Mindset

Being a power user isn't about mastering every feature. It's about shaping habits that maintain your momentum and relying on the system you've built. Power users don't log into Noda and wait for inspiration. They step in with intention. They know what map they're building, where to begin, and how to keep momentum alive.

Some treat their maps as living journals, updating them daily. Others build frameworks and reuse them as templates. Many work with Conversational AI to uncover connections they might have missed. The details vary, but the mindset is the same: each person has shaped Noda into a space that reflects how they think.

That's the real power of the tool. You don't just make maps. You map the way you think. Once your system becomes second nature, every session starts quicker, runs deeper, and ends with more clarity than a flat screen can offer.

Take Action

Noda isn't just another virtual tool. It's a space where you can move, connect, and shape ideas in three dimensions. The best way to learn is to explore. Try out different environments, test the features, and see how they support the way you think.

Once your account is set up, start with a simple map. Build a story outline, organize a concept, or sketch out your next project. Notice how the space itself influences your process.

You don't have to create in isolation. Join Noda's Discord where users share maps, trade tips, and post ideas. The more you connect, the more you'll discover.

Get the Noda app. Make a map. Experiment, adjust, and keep going. Turn sparks into patterns, patterns into projects, and projects into something real.

Stay Connected

If this book sparked something for you, I'd love to hear about it. I read every review. You can share your thoughts where you picked up the book or on Goodreads, and your words help other readers discover Noda too.

Want updates on immersive tools, creative workflows, and new book releases? You've got options:

- Sign up for the newsletter at www.michaelawirtz.com for early launch announcements, giveaways, and curated resources.
- Subscribe to my Substack for reflections on creativity, VR writing, holistic wellness, and more.
- Curious about indie publishing? Visit the blog: michaelawirtz.com/blog

For real-time updates and behind-the-scenes posts:

- Facebook: facebook.com/M.E.WrightAuthor
- Instagram: instagram.com/michaela_reikimom

Your next map is waiting. Let's see where your ideas take you.

Acknowledgements

Many thanks go to Rick for much-needed and repeated sanity checks. It's incredible working with you. Janusz, your final tweaks to the cover mean everything to me! And, to Brian: you created an awesome app that helped me stay focused through several fiction books.

To my beta readers: I deeply appreciate your feedback and patience as we edited this project. Every idea and change you suggested helped me move from spark to publication!

FAQ

Is there a way to move an entire group of nodes at once?
Yes. First connect the nodes together, then collapse them into the main (parent) node. Place the circle inside a node, hold the trigger, and drag to another node to form a link. Once all are linked, collapse them into the parent, then place the circle inside that node and press the wrist trigger to move the whole group.

When I collapse my node group, it doesn't fully close. Some nodes stay visible. Why?
This usually happens when the links were created out of order. For collapsing to work correctly, each link needs to start from the main (parent) node. If you notice stragglers that won't collapse, relink them to the parent and try again.

How do I select a group of nodes?

Place the circle inside one of the nodes and press A. The node flashes to confirm. Hold the trigger and draw a ring around the nodes you want. A white outline appears as you go. Release to confirm, then press the trigger again to open the group menu. From there you can rename, recolor, reshape, add notes, or apply the same image across all nodes.

How can I view my map on my phone or laptop?
Export the map. You'll receive an email with a link that opens on your phone, tablet, or computer.

Can I make changes to my map outside of Noda?
Yes. The only way to edit a map outside the app is by exporting it as a CSV file.

- Export: Open the in-app menu, go to Maps, choose your map, and click Export (CSV). Enter your email to get a link and a CSV file.
- Edit: Open the CSV in a spreadsheet editor to rename nodes, rearrange items, or bulk edit.
- Import: Save the updated file to cloud storage, then use Noda's Browser to download and reopen it in your workspace.

Is there a hand-tracking tutorial?
No. Hand tracking depends on your headset's built-in features.

Teleporting isn't working when I point and pull the trigger. What should I do?
This may be a bug. Restart Noda to ensure you're running the latest version, then check your internet connection. If the problem continues, submit a report with a short video or screenshots in the **#bug-report** channel.

Can I copy part of a map into another one?
Not directly. You can import a full map into another map, then delete the parts you don't need.

I'm in a shared map with both Free and Plus users. Will the 50-node limit apply?
Yes. Shared sessions default to the lowest tier. If a Free user is present, the limit is 50 nodes for everyone.

Can I carry a node while I move around? Dragging it across the room takes too long.

Yes, but it's manual. Collapse your structure so you only move one node, hold it with one hand, and teleport with the other.

Can I buy a specific environment like the Glasshouse without subscribing?

Not at this time. If the option is added in the future, only new environments would be sold individually.

Is it safe to log into my Google account with the in-app browser?

Yes. Your login data is stored locally on your headset.

How do I replace a node shape with an image?

Using the Image Library

To add an image, start by creating a new node and include a description of the image you want to display. You can choose an image from the Image tab, generate one using the Brain, or find one through the Page tab.

Dragging from the In-App Browser

Open the browser, find the image you want, and drag it directly onto the map. This creates a new node with the image as its base.

I can't subscribe to Noda Plus on my iPhone. What should I do?

Try completing the purchase inside Noda on your Meta Quest headset. Open the menu, go to Upgrade, and approve the subscription with the card linked to your Meta account. If that fails, confirm your payment method is current or try again later in case the App Store is experiencing issues.

I cannot press the Account button. What should I do?

This usually happens when the Import folder on your headset is full, which pushes the Account tab off the bottom of the panel. If you have a USB connection to a PC, clear the folder at: Android\data\com.codingleap.noda\files\Import.

After you clear the folder and restart Noda, the extra tabs will disappear and the Account tab will be accessible again.

What features are available for each headset Noda supports?

Hand Tracking: Native on Quest; limited support on SteamVR depending on hardware.

Finger Tracking: Supported by Valve Index controllers.

Body Tracking: Quest supports emulated upper-body tracking through Virtual Desktop; SteamVR supports full-body tracking with accessories like Vive Trackers.

Eye Tracking: Built into certain headsets (e.g., Vive Pro Eye, Varjo VR-3).

Facial Tracking: Available with the HTC Vive Facial Tracker.

Feature	Meta Quest Series	HTC Vive	SteamVR-Compatible Headsets
3D Mind Mapping	Supported	Supported	Supported
Hand Tracking	Supported	Limited[1]	Limited[1]
Passthrough Mode (AR)	Supported	✗ Not Supported	✗ Not Supported
Speech-to-Text	Supported	Supported	Supported
AI Image Generation	Supported	Supported	Supported
Multi-User Collaboration	Supported	Supported	Supported
Physical Keyboard Support	Supported	Supported	Supported
Web Browsers Within App	Supported	Supported	Supported
Virtual Environments	Supported	Supported	Supported
CSV Import/Export	Supported	Supported	Supported
AR Passthrough Portals	Supported	✗ Not Supported	✗ Not Supported
Finger Tracking	Supported	Supported[2]	Supported[2]
Body Tracking	Supported[3]	Supported[4]	Supported[4]
Eye Tracking	✗ Not Supported	Supported[5]	Supported[5]
Facial Tracking	✗ Not Supported	Supported[6]	Supported[6]

For the most accurate and up-to-date information on hardware compatibility and feature support, please refer to Noda's official documentation and release notes.

Quick How-to Guide

Every map starts with a few simple moves. Master these basics and you'll be ready to build, connect, and reshape ideas in Noda.

Navigation and Controls

Open In-App Menu: press the **B-button** on the right-hand controller.

Select a Node or Group of Nodes: press the **A-butto**n on the right-hand controller and draw a circle around the nodes to select.

Undo a Recent Action: Press the **Y-button** on the left-hand controller.

Collapse a Node Group: Place the white circle inside of the main node and press the X-button on the left-hand controller.

Move or Rotate: Use the thumbsticks on either controller.

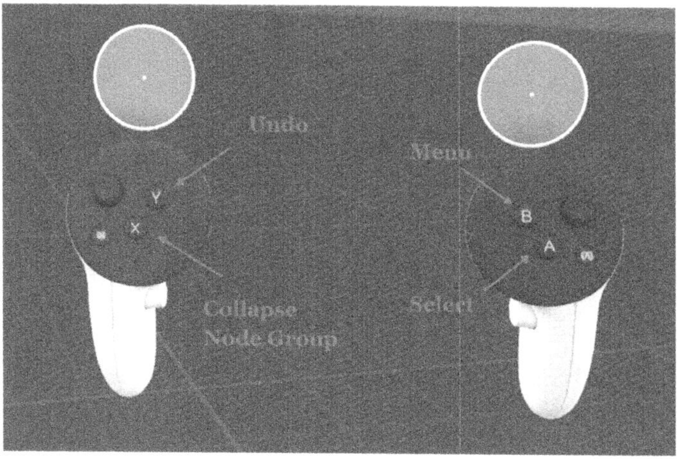

Node Actions

Create a Node: Point the white circle where you want the node and press the **upper trigger**.

Name a Node: Touch the node with the white circle and squeeze/release the trigger. Use the virtual keyboard to type, or hold the trigger and speak to use voice recognition.

Connect Nodes: Place the white circle inside the main node, squeeze the trigger, drag to a second node, and release.

Edit a Node: Place the white circle inside the node and squeeze the **upper trigger** to open the in-app sub-menu (color, shape, notes, web links).

Move a Node: Place the white circle inside the node, use the **grip trigger** and drag it to a new spot.

Resize a Node: Place the white circles for both hands inside the node. Use **both hands with the grip trigger** to enlarge or shrink.

Delete a Node or Connection: Place the white circle into the node, pull the thumbstick back until the pointer turns black, then press the trigger.

Reposition Menus: Place the white beam on the side of the menu. Then, grab the menu, browser, or keyboard with the **grip trigger** and move it where you want.

Voice Recognition: Place the white circle into the node, hold the trigger, and talk. (Only available if your headset has speech-to-text enabled.)

Appendix A: Supported Platforms and Input Devices

Noda runs on multiple VR platforms, but support and features vary. Use this guide to check what works on your headset and how to get the best setup.

Supported Platforms

- **Meta Quest (2, Pro, 3)**: Primary version of Noda. Fully supported, updated regularly, and includes the complete feature set: conversational AI, in-app web browser, speech-to-text, group selection, collapse/expand, and more.

- **Oculus Rift (PCVR, discontinued)**: Runs only in legacy mode. Requires a gaming PC and uses an older build with limited features. No longer updated.

- **SteamVR Headsets (HTC Vive, Vive Pro, Valve Index)**: Runs smoothly with precise tracking.

Passthrough video, AI tools, and the in-app browser are not supported.

- **Windows Mixed Reality (WMR)**: Works through the SteamVR bridge app. Same functionality as other SteamVR headsets, with the same feature limitations.
- **Pico Headsets**: Not officially supported. Some users report partial success with third-party tools, but performance is inconsistent and unsupported.

PCVR Limitations

Not available in PCVR builds:

- Pinch-to-edit
- Conversational AI assistant
- AI image generation
- Undo
- Group selection
- Collapse/expand

Controller note: On PCVR headsets, the upper thumb buttons bring up the in-app menu. The lower thumb buttons are not mapped.

Keyboard Input

Typing with the virtual keyboard works for short edits but is slow and error-prone. A physical keyboard is strongly recommended.

- **Meta Quest**
    - *Bluetooth:* Go to Settings → Devices → Bluetooth → Pair Keyboard.
    - *USB:* Connect with a USB-C adapter.
    - *Tip:* QWERTY layout is the most reliable. Other layouts may cause issues.
- **SteamVR (Vive/Index)**
    - Connect the keyboard to your PC via USB or Bluetooth.
    - Works by default.
    - For better text visibility, use an overlay such as Logitech Bridge.
- **Windows Mixed Reality (WMR)**
    - Install SteamVR and the WMR bridge app.
    - Once set up, launch Noda from your Steam library.

Controllers

Meta Quest Touch Controllers: Fully supported with standard mappings (see Quick Start Guide in this book).

Vive Wand Controllers:

- Trigger: Select or grab
- Grip: Alternate functions
- *Note:* Button mapping may vary by headset model. See Noda's support documentation for details.

Platform Recommendation

Meta Quest (2, Pro, 3) offers the most complete and current version of Noda, with full access to AI tools, the in-app browser, speech-to-text, and the latest updates.

Troubleshooting Checklist

Noda will not launch on SteamVR or WMR

- SteamVR: Confirm SteamVR is installed and running.
- WMR: Confirm the bridge app is installed.
- All PCVR: Try launching Noda directly from your Steam library.
- All PCVR: Update GPU drivers.
- All PCVR: Restart the headset and SteamVR, then try again.

Keyboard input is not working

- Quest: Check Bluetooth pairing in Settings → Devices → Bluetooth, or connect via USB-C.
- Quest: Use QWERTY layout for best results.
- SteamVR: Confirm the keyboard is connected to your PC via USB or Bluetooth.
- PCVR: Check that your operating system recognizes the keyboard in other apps.
- WMR: Confirm SteamVR and the WMR bridge are active.

AI features are missing

- Quest: Confirm you are using a Quest headset.
- PCVR: AI tools are not available on Rift, Vive, Index, WMR, or Pico.
- This is a platform limitation, not a bug.

In-app browser is unavailable

- Quest: The browser is included.
- PCVR: The browser is not supported in PC-based builds.

Controllers feel mis-mapped

- Quest: Reset controller bindings in headset settings.
- SteamVR/WMR: Check default binding profiles in

SteamVR.

- Vive Wands: Confirm trigger and grip mapping in SteamVR.
- All PCVR: If issues continue, restart SteamVR or reinstall bindings.

For the best experience, use Noda on Meta Quest (2, Pro, or 3), where all features are supported and updated. PCVR builds such as Rift, SteamVR, WMR, or Pico can run Noda, but functionality is reduced and troubleshooting is more common.

Appendix B: Console and Integration WebAPI

THIS APPENDIX IS INTENDED for advanced users. Most writers, content creators, and educators will never need to use the Console or Integration WebAPI, and you can safely skip ahead without missing anything essential. These tools exist for debugging, experimenting with custom scripts, or connecting external tools to Noda. If you've ever wanted to "pop the hood" on your map, this is where you'll look.

In this appendix, "Integration WebAPI" and "Integration API" both refer to the same capability. It's exposed to web pages loaded inside Noda's built-in browser through the **noda.js** script.

The Console

What it is: The Console is a small panel inside the VR app that shows live log messages from a web app running in Noda's built-in browser. It also provides controls for restricting which web locations are allowed to call Noda's Integration WebAPI.

Where to find it: In the VR app, open the **Application Menu → Settings tab**. Use the Console toggle to open the panel.

What you see: Once enabled, the Console appears as a floating panel in your workspace. It displays log messages and other output from your running web app. Use it to confirm that your page is loading **noda.js** correctly and that your API calls are reaching Noda.

Security controls: By default, all URLs are permitted to call the Integration WebAPI. You can tighten this by using the Console to block all locations, then allow only the ones you choose. This allowlist approach is recommended for production use or public demos.

Typical use cases: You can use the Console to debug and monitor your web app while it runs inside Noda, to test Integration WebAPI calls such as creating, updating, or deleting nodes and links, and to confirm that event handlers are firing when users interact with the map.

Integration WebAPI Overview

The Integration WebAPI allows a normal web page—written with HTML, CSS, and JavaScript—to run inside Noda's Chromium-based browser and interact with the live 3D map. Your page includes the **noda.js** script, which exposes methods for creating, updating, deleting, and listing nodes and links, as well as subscribing to events from the VR scene.

How it feels in VR

Your page appears alongside Noda's native UI. Supported inputs include the dual controller pointers, the virtual keyboard, a paired physical keyboard, and speech-to-text.

Recommended Workflow

Start by cloning the starter kit from GitHub, then host the page at an accessible web location. If needed, restrict WebAPI access using the Console. Finally, open the page in Noda's in-app browser and test it with the Console open.

Details

Clone the starter: Use the official starter kit to see a working example. It includes *simple.html*, which demonstrates forms for creating, updating, and deleting nodes and links, as well as handling scene events.

Host your page: Place your page on a host that the headset can reach. Static hosting works well. Pick an option that lets you update files quickly so you can iterate during development.

Enable or restrict access: By default, all URLs can call the WebAPI. For tighter control, open the Console in **Application Menu → Settings** and limit access to only your chosen locations.

Open the page in Noda: Launch the Browser from the Application Menu and load your page. Keep the Console panel visible while you test so you can watch log output and confirm API calls.

Quick Start Example

Here's a minimal HTML page. Replace placeholders with your own content.

```
<!doctype html>
<html>
<head>
<meta charset="utf-8">
<meta name="viewport" content="width=device-width,
initial-scale=1">
<title>Noda Integration WebAPI Demo</title>
<script src="noda.js"></script>
</head>
<body>
<h1>Noda Integration Demo</h1>
<button id="makeNode">Create Node</button>

<script>

document.getElementById('makeNode').addEventListener('clic
k', async () => {
const node = await window.noda.createNode({
title: 'Hello Noda',
color: '#3366ff',
shape: 'Box',
size: 6,
location: { x: 0, y: 1.5, z: -2, relativeTo: 'User' },
notes: 'Created from Integration WebAPI'
});
console.log('Created node', node.uuid);
});
```

```
window.noda.onNodeCreated = function (node) {
console.log('Node created:', node.uuid);
};
</script>
</body>
</html>
```

Open this page inside Noda and watch the Console for your console.log output.

Integration WebAPI Reference

Methods

- createNode(properties)
- updateNode(uuid, properties)
- deleteNode(uuid)
- listNodes(properties)
- createLink(properties)
- updateLink(uuid, properties)
- deleteLink(uuid)
- listLinks(properties)
- getUser()

Events

- onNodeCreated(node)

- onNodeUpdated(node)
- onNodeDeleted(node)
- onLinkCreated(link)
- onLinkUpdated(link)
- onLinkDeleted(link)

Node properties
uuid, title, color, opacity, shape, imageUrl, notes, pageUrl, size, location, selected, collapsed

Link properties
uuid, fromUuid, toUuid, title, color, shape, size, selected

User properties
userId (unique to installation/headset)

Troubleshooting Checklist

- **Console doesn't appear:** Open **Application Menu → Settings → Console**.
- **Page loads but calls fail:** Make sure **noda.js** is included, and verify the page's origin is allowed.
- **Events aren't firing:** Ensure event handlers are set before triggering.
- **Cannot reach page:** Confirm the URL is publicly accessible.
- **Performance is sluggish:** Simplify assets and logic in

your web app.

Best Practices

- Keep the Console open while testing.
- Use test rooms for experiments.
- Restrict WebAPI origins before sharing a headset.
- Version your web app and track changes.

Reference Links

- Official Integration WebAPI documentation: https://noda.io/documentation/webapi.html
- Developer Starter Kit on GitHub: https://github.com/nodaadmin/Noda-Integration-API

Summary

The Console gives you visibility and control over Integration WebAPI access while your page runs inside Noda. The WebAPI itself provides straightforward methods for creating and linking nodes, reacting to user actions, and building XR data visualizations with standard web technologies. Use the

Console for monitoring and security, and use the starter kit to move from idea to demo quickly.

About the Author

Michaela Wirtz is a nonfiction author, tech enthusiast, and lifelong DIYer who blends curiosity, creativity, and real-world tools to help readers unlock their own potential. Whether she's mind-mapping in virtual reality, interpreting the language of dreams, or making herbal salves in her kitchen, Michaela approaches every subject with a balance of intuitive insight and practical application.

Her work spans five creative threads:

VR & Creativity: Use virtual reality to reimagine writing, brainstorming, and project planning

Dream Journaling: Explore dreams as a tool for clarity, insight, and self-discovery

Herbal Wellness: Make herbal remedies and aromatherapy blends that support natural living

Letting Go & Inner Freedom: Create space for peace and transformation through intentional living

New Authors: Grounded, experience-based advice for writers just starting out

You can explore her writing and creative tools at ReikiMom.Substack.com or get author resources at MichaelaWirtz.com.

Also by Michaela

DIY Herbal Book Series

DIY Herbal Spa: Learn How to Make Organic Aromatherapy Bath Products at Home

DIY Aromatherapy: Transform Your Home into an Aromatic Retreat

VR Apps for Writers

Immersed: Transform Your Writing Process with VR

Plot, Plan, Create: Noda Is Your Virtual Writing Companion

A Gift From Morpheus

Into Dreamland: A Practical Guide to Dream Recall, Interpretation, and Lucid Awakening (4Q25)

Dreamland Companion: A Guided Journal for Reflection, Self-Discovery, and Transformation (4Q25)

Midnight Musings: A Dream Anthology

Made in the USA
Monee, IL
24 November 2025

36062873R00056